Herb the Spinning Hamster

Meet Herb the Spinning Hamster.

Wee!

He zooms and spins near planets and stars.

Herb helps if bad things happen.

Never fear if I am near!

Rocket Dog frightens Comet Cat.

Zoom!

I will get you!

Never fear! I am near!

Fox frightens all of the moon rabbits.

Hop!

Hop!

Hop!

Help!

Clear off, Fox!

Thank you, Herb!

Herb sees a big monster.
It is sure to attack!

I am going in!

Grrr!

I will trap you!

That is not fair. You are bigger than me!

Herb is quick.
He nips the monster.

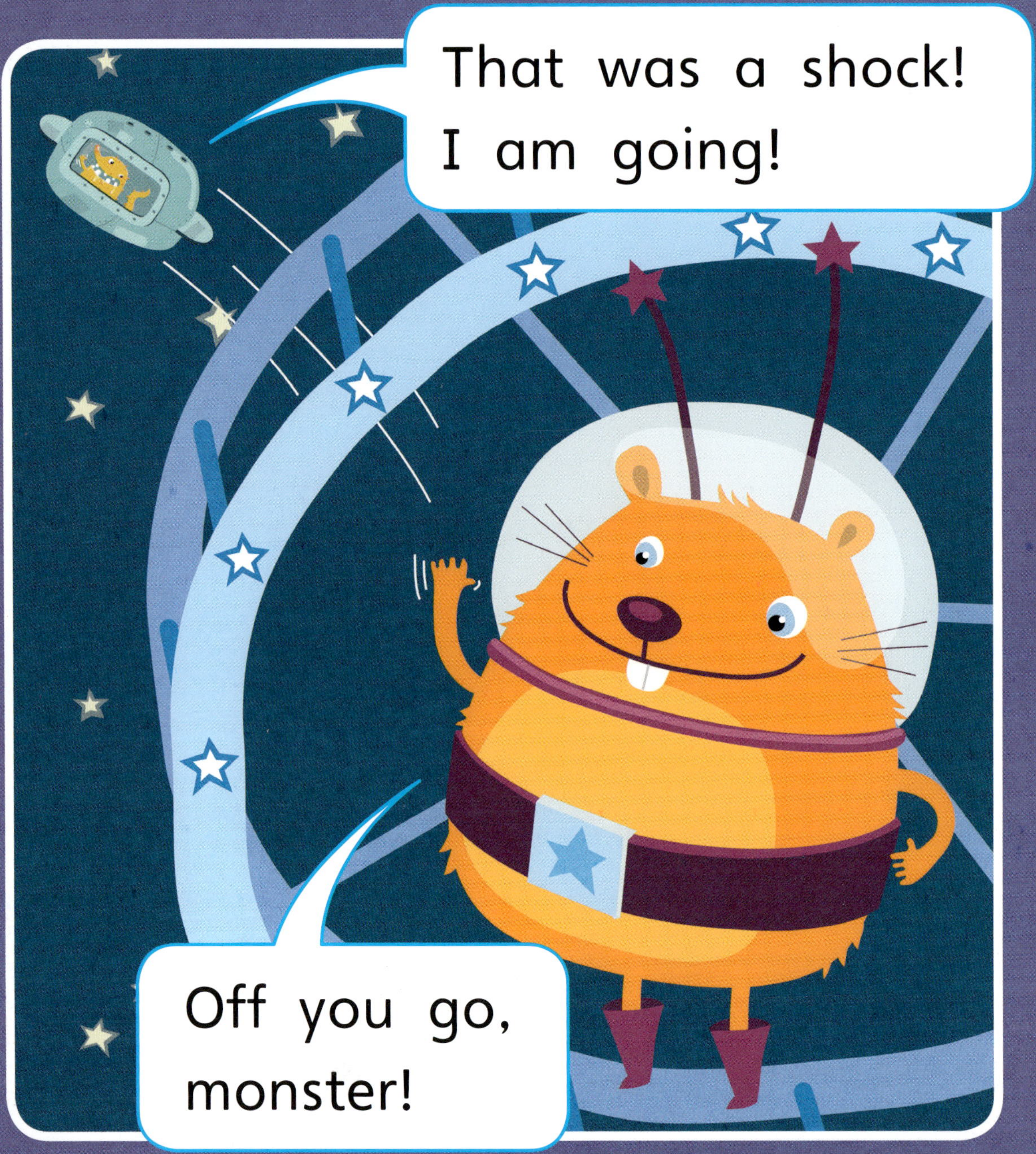
That was a shock! I am going!
Off you go, monster!